Major

You're My Everything

Minor ♪

S.Rivers

My friend, my lover, my wife, you hold
every title vital to me and so much more.
You are my last wish that quickly became
my first. Simply put, you are the reasons that
I love

I can tell you a lot about love because I have
experienced a lot of heartaches and pain. **(I
say again)**
I can tell you a lot about love because I have
experienced a lot of heartaches and pain.

I have cried more tears than the river of
Jordan but having you in my life has made
every tear worth it. You were the hopes &
dreams that never let me give up on love
even when I felt that love had given up on
me. Loving you is not the easiest thing for
me to do, but I still do it willingly without a
second thought.

Thank you for giving me someone to share
all this love that others took for granted
**Your love is the blessing that makes me
forever grateful**

At times, I find myself more grateful than my words could ever reveal, Yet I keep trying to find ways to show you how I truly feel inside. Just to show you half of everything you mean to me, I would need one moment, two hearts & a couple of forever's to show you all the ways that I love, honor & respect you as my woman. **(I say again)**
I would need one moment, two hearts & a couple of forever's to show you all the ways that I love, honor & respect you as my woman.

What you mean to my life

Table of Content

Let Us Begin.

You are the reason that I am inspired to bring the pen back to the paper in hopes of getting closer to your heart. Your love leaves me with great expectations that I gladly accept the challenge.

You move me in ways that make me fall deeper and deeper in love with you. Even if I wanted to, I could never deny what your presence means to my life. When these words reach your heart, I hope that they are received with the love and passion they delivered.

My Friend

Today I want to talk about tomorrow, so tomorrow we can talk about today. The day that you walked into my life was when both of my wants and needs became one. One mind, one heart, and one soul; your love makes me whole.

I need you to know that everything before you were just everything before you. It is my goal to make sure that as your man that I never put anything before you.

You happened to me with no regrets, and I am forever grateful. In your every imperfection, I see the perfection that makes me love you even more. I Love You.

I love you for all the reasons that a man should genuinely love a woman. You complete me. My life became yours the moment you smiled at me.

If ever you should wonder what I offer in your life, this you should know. I am the here and now who wants to be forever when it comes to us. I am not easily broken but fragile when it comes to my heart and emotions. I am the action when words no longer do.

You can have my love. My time and my soul but will you accept my pain, my fears, and my tears. I am far from perfect, but I am even further from being the man who would not put you first in my life. For everything that I am not, I am.

You are not the only one falling in love and are scared.

I have been hurt one too many times for my heart to love so blindly, but my soul keeps reminding me that it only takes one time to get it right. I don't know what tomorrow will bring, so today, I will love you like there is no tomorrow, fearless.

My soul trembles at the mere thought of you not being in my life. When it comes to my life, you matter more to me than me. In my mind, more to me is us, and the only thing more remarkable than us could only be trust. This is what it is going to take for us to see tomorrow together.

My Lover

Here I stand. I stand by every noun and
every verb in the words I love you. Because
I love you, you are more important to me
than my first love simply because you are
my last true love. You are my last wish, my
last chance, and my last opportunity to get
love right finally. As I write these words, my
soul cries out in joy.

I see heaven, the stars above, and all the
wonders of this beautiful world just by
staring into your eyes.

You are the dream that I dream with my eyes
wide open, and this is the first of many
moments that I will take to make sure that I
am doing whatever it takes to keep a smile
on your face.
I knew the moment that I met you that you
would surely be the beginning and end of
my happiness as well as the joy and the pain
of my love. Therefore, I love you. When you

look at me, your eyes speak words that make my soul listen.

Darling, I don't always know how I feel, but I know that I feel something when I am with you. What I think is a feeling that tells me that the giddy feeling in my heart has been replaced with a feeling in my soul that I have always longed for.

Your smile and your love touch me in ways that make me yearn for the touch of your hands. I love you. I love you to the point where it brings me fear. These are the words that go unsaid when I am in your presence, but my soul refuses to remain silent.

I tremble at the thought that this love could break my heart, but I don't care. I would rather die than not have you in my life.

I feel empty when I am not with you for one simple reason. I love you. You are the center of my life that makes me whole. Any and everything necessary to me now begins and ends with you.

No longer does my heart roam because it has now found a home in your soul. Your love gives me life, so I live for the honor to one day make you my wife.

Your love is the promise, promise that makes me want to promise you forever because I would never want to live without you being in my life. Now the question is, could you one day see yourself being my wife. No one can ever come between you and me but us.

My wife,
You should know that when random thoughts are just not random thoughts when my fears sometimes seem to outweigh my hopes when it comes to us, there will always be one thought that gives me peace of mind.

Our Love.
These words say everything, even when you

say that I do not say anything. If I were looking for an easy transition, I would have never let you into my soul because you have captured my heart and don't mind.

My Dear Wife, I have lived a lifetime in these precious moments with you. But still, you have me wanting more. I love you. You should know why I love you will never outweigh the fact that I do.

I love you in every language, using every noun and every verb. Even with no words, I could express to you how I feel. Because of you, I feel loved.

When you smile, I smile because the Most High can now rest; his job is finished. I promise, promise to love, honor, and respect you even after my demise. I may not always be the man you want, but I will always be the man you need to stand by your side.

For me, the puppy love vanished when my soul told me that it was time to embrace my future wife. I have been doing things to make sure that we both deserve to have that other person in their life.

You need to know that my life before you were to prepare me for the day that we would meet. At that moment, one thing became evident to me. I would do whatever it took to keep you in my life. No words can describe the way I feel when it comes to you.

When it comes to you, words like honor, love, and obey will only come second to the words "I do." I vow to you that your every want will be my every need.

When it comes to us, what's on my mind will always reflect what is in my heart. What is in my heart will always speak from my soul. I stand by these words because I love you.

Wow!!!

I love how the words I love you sound when they leave my lips and speak to your soul. Your love makes love possible while our love makes nothing seem impossible, and that is enough for me.

I must admit that I would like to tell you that I am strong enough to deal with whatever we may face in our future together, but I patiently wait for the opportunity to show you that I am ready.
Come what may, I want you at your worse so that I can feel that I deserve you at your best. The only consistency that I need in my life is your love for me.

I know that you are trying to make sense of everything going on in your life, but it is not adding up right now. I want to go on the record and say that I want to be there by your side to help you connect the dots. More importantly, I want to be there to watch you chase away the clouds with your effort.

You are stronger than any obstacle you may face in your life because you will never have to face them alone with me by your side.

In your words, I find the answers to every question. In your heart, I found the place worthy of my love.

For this, I thank you. You are everything that I could ever imagine a woman to be. I digress; you are everything that matters to me. You are my here, and now that makes me want forever when I think about us. You are my happiness. I don't know what tomorrow will bring, so today I will love you like there is no tomorrow with all my soul.

Thank you for allowing me into your life.

When you wake up this morning, I need you to know that you are loved, wanted, and respected in that order. For us to see tomorrow together, we must plan today. Therefore, I intend today to do whatever it takes to keep you in my life. In your darkest hours, in your moments of despair, I will be right by your side.

When those voices in your head are at it loudest, I pray that the voice in your heart refuses to let me go. Whenever, however, and wherever, I will go to be by your side. All I want is you. When it comes to you, all my wants are replaced with all my needs.

Therefore, I say, all I need is you.

From wants to need, need to want; one thing will always remain the same; it is you. Tell me what to do, tell me what to say to reach you, and it's done. I am just trying to find your heart in hopes that I will discover your soul along the way.
You are my happiness, my love, and my pain; therefore, I promise, promise that I will not complain. **(Good morning, my Dear)**

My heart is ready for the love & the pain simply because you are the happiness that I find in both…

As I thumb through the pages of my life, I have discovered one thing to be true. You are the beginning and the end of my story. In my account, as I scribble through the joys and the pain, I find happiness.

Every meticulous detail is highlighted with X's & O's when it comes to us. When it comes to us, this becomes a love story.

Each word, each page, and every chapter are about you, simply because I am madly in love with you. You are my four seasons because I simply refuse to fall.

I will never fall short of loving you.

Your love speaks to me, which is why I listen. I listen because you fill the void in my heart that makes me whole. Your hands hold my heart because your love controls my soul. I would not have it any other way. Just the way you look at me makes me feel that what I feel is enough. **(I say again)**

Just the way you look at me makes me feel that what I feel is enough.

I feel that we could be anything because you are everything necessary in my life. I know to be true. Each time I look into your eyes, I know:

- I can;
- I will;
- End of the story but let me continue our story.

I feel no words should go unspoken. Still, I wonder, do my words say all the things that my soul would say if my soul could speak; Therefore, I tell.

I wish that I could ask you, have you ever, because I never want to know what it feels like to lose you.

(I say again)

I wish that I could ask you, have you ever, because I never want to know what it feels like to lose you.

(Just in case I was not clear, let me say it again)

I wish that I could ask you, have you ever, because I never want to know what it feels like to lose you.

What I am trying to say is that even with nothing, I have something in you.

(Love)

You are the best part of us that makes me whole. I stand before you a better man. Please don't ask me how, but I do know that it is because of you.

Something about you has a hold on me, and I refuse to let go. So, where we go from here is totally up to you. My heart is yours.

You make me want even when I know that I don't need it. You make me feel even when pain is all that I feel inside. I know that it's complicated, but if given time, it will all be clear.

My Dear, my life is filled with so many ups and downs, yet you always find a way to keep me centered. Like a moth to a flame, you will surely be my demise; yet my heart is yours. I love you.

Why I love you is not the question; it is merely the answer to my every question. Why I need you in my life is a statement that I will never question. So why should anyone doubt the way that you make me feel?

The way that you make me feel fills my heart with joy. Need I say more?
How I feel is how I should feel when you know that you are in love, and I know that I am in love with you. I wonder do you know that you are the blessing in every lesson that I learned when it comes to love and pain.

With these words, I say, I feel enough to know that I don't feel enough. I need enough to know that I don't want enough when it comes to us. You are all that matters and to me, which is the only thing that matters in my life.

My wife, my heart is ready for the love and the pain simply because you are the happiness that I find in both.

If I never told you, I am saying it now.
I love you, but more importantly, I need you in my life.

When was the last time that I told you what you mean to my life?

For all the reasons that don't need a reason, allow me to proceed.

I love you... I love you... I love you...
I am hoping as each day passes, those feelings will grow.

I need you... I need you... I need you...
I'm praying that as my feeling grow that my words will finally show.

I want my words to show that I will never turn away even when I can't stand to look at you. Even God knows that not even death could ever keep me away.

Away from you, away from us, away from love.

What I am trying to say with words is that you mean everything to my life that I don't want to lose without a fight.

When it comes to you, I don't want anything because you always give me everything I need. I don't need it simply because I have you in my life. I love you entirely because you complete me in every way.

Never have I felt the way that I felt the first time that I starred in your eyes. I knew from the first time that it would be the last time I fell so deeply in love. Why I love you doesn't change the fact that I do.

(Completely)

You are imperfect, as am I, but that is what I love about you. I love all the little things that make being with you a challenge that I gladly embrace…

I don't want ever to let you go because if you leave, I will surely follow.

My love, I find you to be beautifully imperfect in more ways than one. You are a remarkable woman. I know that I don't say these words often enough, but I won't let another minute pass that these words are not spoken from my lips and softly received by your soul.

You possess qualities that make extraordinary women seem ordinary in your presence.

As I stand before you, I declare, I will never promise you anything, but I will always give you everything I must offer.

My love for you is undeniable. My feelings and emotions are for you to you and not everything else.

(I say again)

My feelings and emotions are for you to you and not everything else.
My love is what you desired, so this is what I humbly give unto you.

You will always be loved, wanted, and needed in my life.
Nothing short of God will ever change the way that I feel about you.

In my darkness, I saw the light, and that
light is you.
In my time of sorrow, I discovered a friend,
and that friend is you.

I'm not where I want to be in my life, but I
hope that it brings me closer to you with
each word.

You make me feel necessary even when you
don't have to do it.

You make the impossible possible in my life
just by being by my side.

Your love gives me what I am worth, which is why you will always have the very best of me.

I am not perfect, but I will always keep trying to be when it comes to you.

Every day with you reminds me that God is able because he has brought his angel into my life.

I love you for the simplest of reasons that words could never express…

Your love compliments me in ways that I choose not to live without in my life.

I'm working on a poem. I am not working on just any poem; I'm working on something to change my melancholy mood into a more acceptable state.

LOVE

When I think about love, thoughts of you come to mind.
In you, I have found the soul mate my arms refuse ever to let go.
You compliment my heart down to my soul.

Most days, I forget why I fell in love with you, but I know that I do every day.
You send me to cloud nine.
From where I stand, the view is immaculate.

You are the sonnet I call a masterpiece.
Your Love is the song I find to be timeless.
In more than just words, you epitomize
beauty.

I love you in a way that warms my soul
when the words 'I love you" are spoken from
my lips.
In any tongue, in every language, my love
for you speaks volumes.

My love,
You hold my attention, like spoken words
from the lips of a poet.
Your love is my stage; your heart is my
audience. Do they find approval in me…?

To me, your love means everything &
nothing.
Everything I live for & nothing short of
being my last breath.

I love you…
I love you in ways that can & cannot explain
in words.

My love for you is a feeling that comes over me every time you walk out that door or say goodbye. I freeze your image in my mind until our next encounter.

As I compose this poem solely inspired by you, I have but one more point to bring to light.

You Move Me

You move me in ways that I want to be guided. Like the wind to sail, I submit to your gentle breeze.

I am far from being a wordsmith but even further from being incapable of bringing my deepest feelings to light.

My words and thought are effortless when it comes to you.
I achieve greatness in life using you as my inspiration.

Somewhere there's a man who's all alone. He is staring at the walls but looking deep within his soul.

He is gazing through the eyes of a lost spirit,
penetrating the mind, trying to hold onto
fading memories.

The closer he assumes he is getting to the
light; each step diminishes that thought.
The end of the journey is not as significant
as the reason.

On this journey, he is searching for
something that has always been there.

Lies are our tools… It allows us to function
in a dysfunctional world.
Dozens of reasons to lie, only one reason to
tell the truth.

I Love you too much not to.
I had known this long before the words" I
love you', were spoken from my lips.
Even with the possibility of me being
wrong, why would I want to be right?

I know where I'm at, but it's not where my
heart wants to be.
I would look at old pictures, but I don't want
to be reminded of everything I'm missing in

my life.
The mere sound of your voice triggers
memories I have been trying unsuccessfully
to suppress.

How can I overcome my current state?
I'm damned if I do, damned if I don't.

My fears of being wrong are stripping me of
all hope.
My desire to be right keeps me moving
mountains in your name.
Your love is the reason for my every action.
I believe in reason above all else.

Many would call me forceful,
I push a noun against a verb to express my feeling
for you.

Many would call me a fool,
I gladly would take a leap of faith to bring us
closer.

The fact remains, even those without eyes can see
how much I Love You.

I love you for the simple things you do.
You're not trying to be Miss Independent.
The only title you desire to obtain is **Mrs**. To my
Mr.

I admire you for the feats I deem impossible.
Accepting me as I am, flaws & all.

As I separate stanzas to solidify the sequence of
words you find to be satisfactory,
I can't help but wonder…

Why

Why have the lights of heaven shinned so bright
on me…?
Why have the gravity of earth pardoned the feet of
my soul…?

Through all my ups & downs, there is only one
constant; we are in this together.
(A great man once said) My feelings for you lie
in each letter that spells my love for you on every
page.

He must have known my wife in a previous life.

You are the Dreams (Dreams) I have while I'm
wide awake.
In the eyes of love, I am a student yearning to be
taught by you alone.
My feet have abandoned my heart's desire to flee.

One often meets his destiny, trying his best to
avoid it.
You are my destiny…

I embrace you by choice & never by force.

Have I ever told you…?

I find beauty in the words that you speak,
which shakes my very foundation.
The sound of your voice is like poetry to my
ears.
The gentleness of your touch warms my
soul, unlike any flame.

You, as a woman, defines true beauty.
(Starting with The Inside Out)

From the moment I met you, all I wanted
was to make you happy.
I loved you so deeply that I surrendered my
emotions until before my mind could
intervene.

If it were not for my mind, my heart would
still be in love with you.
I could never begin to understand
everything, but I overstand this.
With you, I have come full circle in both

love & life.

If you could listen to your heart, you would know.
All I ever wanted was to be a part of your life.
(Forever would have been enough for me)
In you, I saw our present, our future & past.

I was willing to stand by your side even when you were wrong.
Past my fears. Past my doubts. Beyond my better judgment.
(I loved you anyway)

I knew loving you with all that I had would only lead to pain.
I thought. I wished. I hoped to love you would not be in vain.
I found it strange when the love of my life has doubts about carrying my last name.

With you, I feel that I'm holding onto a dream that only I share.
I whisper your name in the wind only to realize that theirs no one there.

I don't think you could ever feel all the Love
I must give.

My definition of love.

A need is so necessary.
A passion is so deep.
Just wanting it could never be enough.
To love is to share a life together for better
or worse. I am not spending another wasted
moment without the person who completes
you.

The person who gives you the strength to
say I do
 (Today-Tomorrow- & Forever) without
any regrets.

The thought of us always being together
gave me life.
I would never have guessed that you had
reservations about being my wife.

My Dearest Love,

If I may, I'm trying to get to know everything about you from the neck up. I don't care about your past because I am your future.

All I want to do is show you how much I love you.

I promise nothing while giving you everything I must offer.

For You, my thoughts kiss words as my lips speak the emotions of my soul.

So, I write words that become speechless
when spoken from my lips unto your soul.

I Love Everything About You.

I needed a way to get it out, so I write it out
with words that make vibrations as my pen
hit the paper. I have learned to love you
empty because I'm wise enough to know that
your love will make me whole.

Starting with today & lasting forever, I want
to engage you, engage you in words that
lead to thoughts that become defined with
action. My actions will become the
foundation of our love.

Through My Heart Felt Words

I love you because I know in return, your
love gives me what I am worth. I fight
myself whenever I tell myself that I'm better
off without you. Loving you makes the
impossible seem possible.

Your love undoes me in more ways than one.
So, I say unto you, shall we proceed because I have not finished yet when it comes to loving you. You mean more to me than words could ever reveal. I know that in time my intents will reflect my feelings.

My love,

The feeling to be heard gives me a strong

motivation to write. So, I attempt to put pen

to paper to inscribe words that break down

the barriers that stand between us.

I need you in ways that have not come full

circle within the confines of my mind. I only

hope that you allow me the time to

determine how important you are to me. I

try to find words that will bring us closer,
even when my actions seem to be pushing us
apart. I find myself finally willing to do the
one thing I should have done from the
beginning; Listen to you

My arrogance has taken everything away
from me that I once deemed essential. I
refuse to let you become the casualty of my
enormous pride. Being without you is a feat
worse than dying. So, I'm trying to do
whatever it takes to keep us together. Your
love is an honor that I refuse to put in my
rearview mirror. If it takes words to start our

reunion process, then I will compose sonnets

until my actions resemble every utterance

spoken unto you. In the past,' I may have

made these same declarations; the one

difference between then and now is that I'm

doing it for us this time. I deem our love

worthy of such a feat.

I had a dream about you last night.
Never have I had a vision that made me feel
grateful that it was not my reality. **(Me
without you)** is one site my eyes find hard
to recognize.

Trying to Hold onto Forever

I hope that I'm one.
I am not the perfect man, but all the man
you'll ever need.

That voice in my head says it's impossible to
put my love for you in words, but still, I try.
I know enough to know that I don't know
much, but I'm willing to learn.
So, I ask, when is your turn.

Before It too late

 My broken mirror, you are the reflection of
my life; I live in the shattered pieces of your

Frame. Your tears torment me; I'm
distraught by your pain. Images of my
failures are driving me insane.

You have always spoken from my heart.
My soul trembles at the thought of you are
not in my life.
From my birth, I knew that you would be
my wife.

I'm better than my worse mistakes.
Nothing in life is too late if patience teaches
you to wait.

They say gratitude knows no limits. When

does my pain grants forgiveness?

Don't let the ceiling block how high you can
rise because your pride will never stop or
prevent your demise.

All it takes is a moment to view me in a
different light.
Close your eyes and allow your soul to give
you that sight.

I'm a better man for losing you, but never
will I consider it a mistake to choose you.

Yes, you are that red rose covered in white
snow,
but I am the sun that gave you the light to
grow.

We have something like a miracle. That
precious gift is forgiveness.
(So, I Have Been Told) I had to search
within your heart to find the love that was
already within my soul.

If you would be so kind,
  Indulge me for a moment, and I will reveal

unto you my deepest thoughts.

If given a chance, I will gladly confess things you may not know to be true. As I speak, I only ask that you listen with your soul.

You are the one that I want; I only desire to be the one that you need in your life. From our first embrace, I found you to be incorrigible.

I believe in many things, but this I know to be true.
I love you. Pick a noun and choose a verb, and I'll give you a word that describes that love.
From A to Z, I will assemble words that your soul will conclude are:
More Than Just Mere Words

You are my sky; my soul takes flight just to be that much closer to you. I envisioned you in my dreams,
never could reality be more beautiful than my thoughts of you.

Even unconscious, my heart proclaims its'
love unto you.
I don't like the fact that I know this, but I am
sure that it's true.

You are right to my evil.
My conscience is dead when it comes to not
loving you.
I live for your love, so I am inanimate when
I'm away from you.

I am perplexed by this revelation but assured
by this one fact.
Unrestricted by doubt, unlimited by fear, I
am meticulous that my love for you is
absolutely the best thing this man should
offer.

As long as I can breathe, I will tell you how
much I Love You.
Emphasis on the I and You, Love is what we
have between us.
I Love You.

I find it unbelievable that another being could love you the way that I do…
Only God himself could relate to such a privilege.

Beyond emotions, my love for you is the heartbeat that gives my soul life.

If only you knew

Right here, Right Now, you have my attention.
You are the center of my life, and that's all that matters.
I don't know what I feel, but I know that I feel something with you.
When I'm with you, I feel the old me dying while the new me is being born with heaven's blessing.
Being with you has always been a plan that was bigger than us.

With every beat of my heart, you should know that I love you. I have put years behind the words "I Love You" with no regrets. You are everything that I consider being important in my life. I fell in love with you from the moment that we met, and I'm still horizontal. I'm willing to lose everything in this world that doesn't consist of you and our love.

At some point, there will be a time that I feel like I can breathe when I'm not with you, but until that day, I will slowly exhale.
Therefore, I say, if there is heaven without

you, I would consider it hell. I can't make you want me no matter how much I need you in my life. I can only tell you the reasons that I want to make you my wife. As I look in your eyes and into your soul, I confess all I want is you. If you knew my heart, you would understand my mind. If you understood my mind, you would grow to love my soul. I digress; all I need is you. What's understood should never have to be explained.

I want to die in your arms and become one with your soul, but I will settle for living inside your love until that day. I'll give you all of me just to make you whole if you would only pause to see that it is my heart and soul that you hold. I offer a love that would change your mind for the woman who wants but doesn't need it. Beyond the depths of our fears, love opens a whole new world.

(I love you) Welcome to my world.

I let go so quickly because I don't know how
to hold onto what I want in my life.
I don't know how to embrace that which I
love like there was no tomorrow.

I don't know how to keep trying even when
the outcome seems pre-destined.

**(My failures as a youth have crippled the
man before you)**

My flaws are numerous, but my desire to
change is more significant.
I know what is needed to make things right;
I only hope to be ready.

Ready to face my challenges, like the
affections of new love.
(Eyes wide shut and head on)

Ready to do the things that will bring us
closer together. **(Love you)**
For so long, you have waited for me to see
the woman that you are.
(I now close my eyes and see the Goddess
before me)

For so long, you have waited for me to speak the words that your spirit has begged to hear. (I say those words with the force that moves mountains and the will that brings us together)

You have excepted me for who I am. (I must now do the same)
I embrace your faults with the love I do for your strengths.
I embrace your emotions with the wisdom I admire right knowledge.

(I respect the will of the father) I now have a deeper overstanding of what he wants. **(I appreciate the needs of my Goddess)**
I now have a greater overstanding of what she needs with great respect and love that is overdue.

I submit to you.
I claim you to be

It is because of you that there is an Us. It is because of trust that there is love. I love you for all the reasons that a person doesn't need a reason to be in love.

I want to give my heart to the person who desires it& pray that it was worth the wait.

I just can't stop thinking about it so let me put it into words.
You touch my heart in ways that my words caress your soul
When I hold you in my arms, in my mind, my heart, and my soul, there is no doubt that you are the one for me.

Who we love is the person that our soul says that we need to love?
Why we love is not more important than the fact that we love it. Who we love is the person our soul says? This is love.
With you in my life is the last time I want to say it's the last time I fall in love.
I look at you, and I can tell that you are someone I do not want to live without in my life.
You can't, and I will not. How long will I

love you; for as long as I love.

I love you from the I to the U in the words I love you, including every letter in-between.

Don't you ever because I will never give you a reason to leave my side.

We should

From major to minor, you are everything in between.

My sun, my moon, my earth; you are my universe.

My lover, my wife, my friend

You give my life both purpose and meaning with your presence; therefore, you are my future.

When I look at you, I know that this is just the beginning.

It has always been that way.

How do you tell a woman you love her…?

(With Actions)

How do you show a woman you love her with all you got?

(With patience)

What do you give a woman who has

everything? **(My Offering is Love)**
What do you do for a woman who is not
satisfied? **(Try Again)**

My love,
Take time to realize I'm trying even when it
seems like I'm not putting forth an effort.
I'm holding onto what I'm feeling inside but
is my love in vain?
Falling in love with you was easy; getting
you to accept us is the hard part.
If I'm the one you always dreamed about,
why won't you let us happen?

My love for you goes beyond pain, fear, &
doubt.
My love is the place your heart can always
call home.

I Love You. Not just today, but always &
forever.
My best defense to the reason why I love
you so much is simple.
(Love is the answer)

I need for you to know that me being in love
with you is not just words.

I'll do whatever it takes to turn this around.
I'm willing to be wrong so that you can be right.
I need you in my life.

I can't explain; I feel it.

I walk the earth, but your love keeps my feet off the ground.
The sound of your voice brings me home in a way I can't explain.
I'm alive when I'm in your presence.

I can't explain; I feel it.

I see the world in your eyes.
I feel the love of heaven within your arms.
Your smile alone makes all my sacrifices worth giving.

You do this to me and even more.
I can't spell it out for you, but if you give me the time, I'll find a way.
(I love You That Much)

I love you with all I got, but I know I can do better.

I can't explain; I just feel it

I can express my feelings for you with four letters making one word. (Love)
Without even trying,
I have come to love you in a way that I utter words that shakes mountains & moves the seas.
Your smile has become the clue that guides me in the direction of seeking my right destination, getting closer to both your heart & soul.
Gravity works against me as I attempt to ascend near the levels of your greatness.
Nevertheless, I am there.
Here I stand, in the place where I was destined to be.

Next to you

I have pictured this moment a thousand
times within my mind, and I am still
amazed.

As I stare into your eyes, there's one thing
for sure; I don't want to lose that view.

I Love You.

I want to spend a lifetime getting to know
everything about you while using a different
lifetime, showing you everything I have
learned.
I want to touch you in ways that let you
know that the declarations I say are valid,
with words & hands that become one when
my fingers caress your skin, like the rays of
the sun.

I declare I have found my happiness in you.
Indeed, you can guess that the words I speak

are real.
From This Day, I pronounce my love for you
in the strongest of terms.

At the conclusion of sounding redundant, I
attempt subtle ways of expressing my
emotions to you.

In love, I have found a way to become
engaged in you from the inside out.
If you could gather from my words that my
intentions are noble,
it would put to rest any & all fears that you
may have.

My feelings for you are the result of being
truly in love as I am with you.
Presuming that you love me, I would hope
in time that you will come to trust me as
well.
I am not without flaws but loving you could
never be one of them.

Major

You're My Everything

Minor ♪

S.Rivers

How Do I Love Thee…? **(For the New Millennium)** Where do I dare to begin:

You are a Goddess who amazes me in more ways than I have taken the time to realize. No longer will I sleep on The Most High's Greatest Gift to Man. **(The Black Woman)**

(I say unto you) I am now wide awake.

(Black Woman)

Irreplaceable, Priceless are just a few of the words that come to mind when I think of you. Respectfully, I say unto thee, let me count the ways that I love you.

(1) Your Mind. **(Amazing)** Often overlooked and always under-appreciated. I cherish more than your beauty, smile, & grace because it is what makes you the one being, I would bow down to without a second thought.

(2) Your Body… **(The Holy Grail)** The actual cup of life. The scientist no longer needs to search for the mother of all living things.
(The Black Woman) Often imitated but never truly duplicated.

(3) Your Soul… **(The accurate measure of

you) The most significant parts of you are invisible to the sense of sight. Even without eyes, your true beauty would be breathtaking.

I speak to you in ways that a man should always talk to his better half. **(With Love)**

I walk this Hell **(Earth)** for one purpose only. **(You)**

If you fall, I would be there to catch you.
If you wonder, I would be there to reassure you.
If you error, I would be there to teach you.

My kingdom would be incomplete without you. Let me say it again:
(Our Kingdom would be incomplete without you)

I was fleeing the one thing I should have been chasing from the beginning.

(Your emotions) I'm tired of losing one moment, not making you happy. You are my destiny. I will no longer pray for the day to make you see how I feel about you. I will simply use each day to show you.

This is how I love thee. Let me say it again: **(This is how much I'm in love with thee)**

Because I love you…

I look at you, and I know that you are the one. You are my first and last thought of the day, which is why it only fits that you are everything in-between.

I love you.

From the moment that we met; my soul screamed those words before my lips could utter a sound.

You are my friend and my lover, but there is one title that remains. When it comes to you, I want anything that begins with you, but my heart needs everything that ends with us.

My Darling, I need you to know; why we love is not more important than the fact that we love. Who we love is the person our soul says; this is love? I want you to understand, but I need you to overstand that you are loved when it comes to you.

In my eyes, but more importantly, in my heart, you are **<u>Somone</u>** Special. When I hold you in my arms, in my mind, my heart, and my soul, there is no doubt that you are the one for me.

You move me in ways that scare me, but still, I stand before you. Even though I don't want to say, I am trying to say that I don't want you ever to doubt me because I will never give you a reason to leave my side.

I make a vow with words the one thing that my soul will now and forever promise, promise unto you. I will always love you. (Even when you make it hard to do so.) I will love you more.

What you mean to me is everything that has
meaning in my life. What you mean to us is why I
want to know if you would be my wife.

(This is the one thing that I am sure of)